CONTENTS

INTRODUCTION

These are historic times in customer service and life. The future seems uncertain, and hope for better days ahead seems to rise and fall like the rollercoaster we are all riding each day.

And yet, there is so much opportunity ahead for us. COVID-19 has caused businesses and individuals to step back, rethink, e-envision and innovate their future.

Many businesses are currently rethinking how they will remain open, or one day be able to reopen. The virus has forced many employees to work from home and…surprise: some businesses are planning to allow them to continue working remotely. Article after article highlights the "light bulb" moments that business leaders are expressing about the death of large office spaces, both in terms of the dollars saved and the convenience of their employees working from home. Employees are enjoying the lack of commutes and less stressful working lives, and businesses are enjoying a better experience for the customer.

As the days, weeks and months of the pandemic continue to go by, one truth remains…as it always has: businesses will rise and fall because of their ability to change and meet the needs of their customer - or not.

As businesses find their new modes of operation and sustainability, another important truth cannot be overlooked: For any business to achieve its goals and mission, they must retain and cultivate new customers.

To help achieve that, I've written this little book of professional customer service. This handy guide will help employees deliver the service customers expect in the age of COVID-19, and will also help employees communicate their needs and wants with their colleagues and co-workers - the internal customers - more effectively.

The pages ahead are filled with information, tips, techniques and questions to assist you, the employee, in assessing and improving your levels of professionalism. Whether you work from home or have returned to your place of work, the purpose of this book is to challenge you to examine your role in customer service and encourage you to choose to be better.

And finally, organizational leaders will find this little book to be of value too, because it will help them to define the future of the customer experience in their businesses through the eyes of their most important asset: their people!

PROFESSIONAL CUSTOMER SERVICE

To provide professional customer service there are three important skills or competencies that employees must learn, continually improve upon, and constantly demonstrate to every customer - including the internal customer. These attributes must be relentlessly supported and honed by the management of the organization.

They are Skills, Good Judgment and Radical Hospitality.

Let's begin with Skills. Many of us working in customer service are experiencing a quickly changing work environment, even without COVID-19. The need to sharpen existing skills and learn new ones is becoming even more important for not only the success of our businesses, but also for our own job satisfaction and security.

There are **Three Skills of Professional Customer Service** that you should be focusing on specifically: technical literacy skills, communication skills, and leadership skills.

Technical Literacy Skills
The first set of skills for you to self-assess are your Technical Literacy Skills.

We live in an age of growing technological dependency. This has become the norm, as most people working in customer service own a smartphone and computer, and many of the daily work tasks are becoming computer enabled or assisted.

With such a prevalence of technology in the workplace, there are basic computer and technology skills that everyone serving customers needs to learn. Going beyond that, they also must show that they know how to use technology to advance their professional performance.

To be a professional, you must continue to master the

technical skills that your position requires. While the applications of technology can vary greatly from position to position, one of the lessons learned from working in the time of COVID19 is that technology is playing a bigger and more integrated role in connecting with, acquiring and serving customers.

Think about the technical skills that are currently required for your customer service position. How has the technology used in your work space changed since the pandemic began? How is your organization planning to incorporate technology in the future to meet the changing business environment?

Some of the basics include becoming proficient in fundamental technology programs such as Microsoft Suite (i.e. Word, PowerPoint, Excel, and Outlook) and being able to navigate search engines - including learning the tips and tricks outside of a basic search in Duck Duck Go or Google.

If you are interested in learning some of the time- and headache-saving tips and tricks of searching in Google, check out the webinar Google Like a Librarian. This is one of my company's (PCI Webinars) most popular programs that you can watch for free just by signing up for our newsletter. This article on Basic Computer Skills is also worth checking out: https://www.saxonsit.com.au/blog/workplace/5-basic-computer-skills-every-employee-should-have/

Now complete the following mini-assessment. Be honest and unafraid of your answers - the goal here is awareness, not self-criticism.

1. What Technical Skills are needed in your position?

2. Which Technical Skills are your greatest strengths?

3. Which Technical Skills do you believe that you can improve?

4. What resources are available to you now that you can utilize to improve the Technical Skills you listed in question #3.

5. Why do you want to improve the Technical Skills that you listed in question #3?

6. What obstacles will you have to overcome to improve those skills?

7. How will you overcome those obstacles?

8. How will you know when you have improved upon those skills?

9. Do you want a co-worker or your direct report to coach and/or support you in improving your skills?

Communication Skills

The next set of skills for you to self-assess are your Communication Skills. To be a professional, you must continue to master the challenging art and skills of communication that your position requires.

An article from FastCompany.com by Jillian Kramer highlights several communication skills that are needed to succeed in the workplace, and I've listed these skills below to demonstrate their importance in delivering professional customer service.

1. Show Respect

The foundation for professional customer service is respect. Without respect for the customer there can be no opportunity to build healthy relationships - which is the lifeblood of any business. Customer service is also situational, meaning that the needs of each customer are different and building respectful relationships with them starts with respecting their needs.

Respect can be seen as a code of conduct, a set of mutually agreed upon behaviors that defines how employees will interact and communicate with one another in order to serve both each other and their external customers. These can include expectations for how they behave, act, speak, interact, email, share, communicate, and/or represent themselves in their workplace.

Before any business can provide professional external customer service, the employees of that organization must first respect one another and the important roles played by everyone. At all levels of the organization, staff must value treating others with respect and civility. Consider the Platinum Rule by Dr. Tony Alessandra:. "Do unto others as they would have done unto them."

2. Actively Listen

Think about a time when you were the customer and you didn't feel like you were heard, or that the customer service employee treated you with indifference instead of interest and respect. Did it make you want to do business with that employee and company?

Customers want to be heard. They want to feel like you **care** about them enough to listen to their concerns, needs and desires. Professional customer service requires continually sharpening your listening skills.

Perhaps the best advice given on actively listening comes from Dr. Stephen Covey in the book the 7 Habits of Highly Effective People: "Seek first to understand, then to be understood."

The goal is to understand the customer. And when you seek to understand them, the customer will feel heard and respected.

And a reminder: You can seek first to understand your customer without agreeing with them.

3. Ask Questions for Clarification

Have you ever had a conversation with a customer who either did not know what they wanted or could not clearly express it? Most people working in customer service would probably answer that question with, "Yes, everyday!".

Now put yourself in the shoes of the customer that is trying to communicate something and appears to be failing; it's frustrating for both of you.

Professional Customer Service requires you to take mental or physical notes while the customer is talking. Don't be afraid to ask the customer if you can write things down – it shows them that you are interested and want to help, and that you can ask the appropriate questions when needed.

There's an art to asking effective questions to get the information that is needed from the customer without escalating the conversation or upsetting them.

Some of my favorite questions to ask for clarifying purposes include:

Did I hear you correctly when you said…?

Is this what you said...?

Did I hear you say...?

Did I understand you when you said...?

Did I paraphrase what you said correctly?

Reminder: Use "I" statements to take ownership of your words and to prevent the customer from getting defensive.

4. Remain Open-Minded and Present

What is one of the most difficult challenges in customer service? For me, it's treating every customer uniquely. Professional customer service means staying open-minded and present with your customer when:

You've heard that question before
You've heard that complaint before
You've dealt with similar situations before

When your thoughts turn to, "Oh, this question again," or, "Not this complaint again," or, "Been there, done that," you are making that customer interaction about you and your experiences. And sorry, it isn't about you!

Remind yourself to be present with the customer as it is likely the first time that they are coming to you with that particular question, complaint or situation. Also, be open-minded to solving their need in ways that you haven't done so previously.

5. Learn to Be Comfortable with Silence

There will be times in your customer interactions where a moment or two of silence will occur. Resist the urge to fill it with words. I remember hearing an interview with Mick Jagger from the Rolling Stones when they asked him about silence in music. Paraphrasing him, he said that if there wasn't silence in music (meaning instruments having to play all the time and singers constantly singing), all you would hear is noise. Furthermore, he said that silence is the key to creating music.

Many people are uncomfortable pausing and giving a moment

or two of silence in a conversation with a co-worker or a customer. Some find that moment of silence to be very awkward. People delivering professional customer service, however, understand that silence can give others space to think, which helps you to be more effective in your work.

Practice using this technique: When someone asks you a question, make it a habit to think for a few seconds before you speak. It shows confidence to be okay with a little bit of silence.

Some customers will perceive that you take their question seriously, but as with everything in professional customer service one size does not fit every customer. If you see that they are uncomfortable or impatient with you taking a second or two to answer, change your approach to respect the needs of that customer.

Now complete the following mini-assessment. Be honest and unafraid of your answers - the goal here is awareness, not self-criticism.

> 1. What Communication Skills are needed in your position?

> 2. Which Communication Skills are your greatest strengths?

> 3. Which Communication Skills do you believe that you can improve?

> 4. What resources are available to you now that you can utilize to improve the Communication Skills you listed in question #3.

5. Why do you want to improve the Communication Skills that you listed in question #3?

6. What obstacles will you have to overcome to improve those skills?

7. How will you overcome those obstacles?

8. How will you know when you have improved upon those skills?

9. Do you want a co-worker or your direct report to coach and/or support you in improving your skills? If yes, who would you choose and why?

Leadership Skills

The final set of skills for you to self-assess are your Leadership Skills.

From tonyrobbins.com, "Leadership is the ability to inspire a team to achieve a certain goal. It's usually discussed in the context of business, but leadership is also how you, as an individual, choose to lead your life. The true leadership definition is to influence, inspire and help others become their best selves, building their skills and achieving goals along the way."

You don't have to be a CEO, manager or even a team lead to be a leader. Leadership is a set of skills – and a certain psychology – that anyone can master."

"The new model of leadership is all about every single stakeholder showing leadership in the work they do." He describes leadership as a "philosophy" and an "attitude," not a position; a, "State of mind … available to each one of us."

Leadership is a mindset where employees focus not on the problem but on finding the solution, where employees all have a personal responsibility to advance the business, and where each employee is able to "shape culture, stay positive, and lead by example".

Benjamin Zander (2000), conductor of the Boston Philharmonic Orchestra, shares a perspective from his musical background: "I had been conducting for nearly twenty years when it suddenly dawned on me that the conductor of an orchestra does not make a sound."

His picture may appear on the covers of CDs in various dramatic poses, but his true power derives from his ability to make other people powerful.

"I began to ask myself questions like, 'What makes a group lively and engaged?' instead of, 'How good am I?'" This is the mindset of a leader.

Now complete the following mini-assessment. Be honest and unafraid of your answers - the goal here is awareness, not self-criticism.

> 1. What Leadership Skills are needed in your position?

> 2. Which Leadership Skills are your greatest strengths?

> 3. Which Leadership Skills do you believe that you can improve?

> 4. What resources are available to you now that you can utilize to improve the Leadership Skills you listed in question #3.

> 5. Why do you want to improve the Leadership Skills that you listed in question #3?

6. What obstacles will you have to overcome to improve those skills?

7. How will you overcome those obstacles?

8. How will you know when you have improved upon those skills?

9. Do you want a co-worker or your direct report to coach and/or support you in improving your skills? If yes, who would you choose and why?

Mastering Good Judgment

About 35 minutes northwest of Detroit, the Wixom Public Library serves a city of more than thirteen thousand residents. The library provides a variety of services to their community, comparable to what many libraries around the country offer. What makes this library stand out is their customer service policy:

"While at work, each staff member is a representative of the library. The impression we make profoundly affects the library's image and ongoing support. Because every patron interaction is important, being helpful is our highest priority. All other library policies should be interpreted in light of the principles outlined below."

<u>**Customer Service Principles**</u>

· Treat every patron with equal respect and every request with equal importance.

· Always be ready and willing to help, making patrons feel valued.

· Provide accurate, friendly and efficient service, and invite patrons to return.

· Do your best to meet patrons' needs and exceed their expectations. Whenever possible, judgment calls should be made in the patron's favor.

· If you are unable to comply with a request, offer an alternative.

· Be well-versed in library policies and be able to explain the rationale behind them.

· Always seek possible improvements to promote service excellence.

How can this public library in a small town "get it", when large companies with multi-million-dollar customer service budgets seem to completely miss the mark on customer service with their training and policies?

"Getting it" means setting the customer-facing employees free to use their own good judgement when it comes to serving the customer.

Employees need to exercise good judgment in customer service because it shows that you will react in an appropriate way when handling even the most unexpected situations.

Part of using good judgment is not overreacting or reacting emotionally in highly tense situations with customers. Customers and employers want to see employees make effective decisions and choices, especially when they are under pressure.

Good judgment also naturally leads to good decision making, and businesses need their employees to make good decisions. Customers have choices, and they are even more likely to look elsewhere if their service expectations are not met because of an employee's poor decision.

Having said that, Professional Customer Service is a team effort. Employees must have the support of management in practicing good judgment, and management must hire people that possess good judgment - and then give their employees the proper training and guidance to succeed.

Another example of creating a culture of "good judgment" is Nordstrom. For years their customer service policy was only 75 words long, and it was printed on a 5 x 8 inch gray card.

Welcome to Nordstrom

We're glad to have you with our Company. Our number one goal is to provide outstanding customer service. Set both your personal and professional goals high. We have great confidence in your ability to achieve them.

Nordstrom Rules: Rule #1: Use best judgment in all situations. There will be no additional rules.

Please feel free to ask your department manager, store manager, or division general manager any question at any time.

You may be thinking, "Surely, they will just give away the store," but most employees are smarter than that, and some customers are more reasonable than that.

Having said that, Nordstrom and the Wixom Public Library understand that Professional Customer Service is not just something that happens without guidance. When judgment calls are made by the employees, they are reviewed and discussed by management not only with the individual, but with everyone in the department, the store and the library.

Making Radical Hospitality a Habit

By radical, don't think wild-eyed, out of control, or in your face. Instead, imagine employees offering the absolute utmost of themselves to others: their creativity, their abilities, and their energy.

Radical means, "Drastically different from an ordinary practice; outside the norm," and so it evokes practices that exceed expectations, that go the extra mile, and that take welcoming the customer to the max.

Radical Hospitality means treating other people fairly and courteously. It means using good manners and appropriate speech, not talking down to your customers or co-workers, and not using profanity or other inappropriate words and phrases.

It is not just words, however, it is also the actions we take with our customers. It means being respectful to everyone, no matter their position or title, their shape, size or their color, whether they are rich or poor, live in a mansion or are without a home, and whether you like them or not - or agree with them or not.

And finally, it means being hospitable and in control even when dealing with distraught and difficult customers. This a highly valuable skill that needs to be practiced daily by everyone serving the customer, which is everyone in the business.

Radical hospitality sends a message beyond, "You are a welcome customer." It says, "We see you and want you to be our customer, no matter who, what, and wherever you are." In short, radical hospitality doesn't just ask, "Do you want to be our customer?" It says, "How can we be the best business for you?"

Radical hospitality needs to be recognized and reinforced by everyone in the organization. The saying, "Behavior that is rewarded is behavior that is repeated," is a cornerstone of radical hospitality. It is also the cornerstone of a lack of professional customer service when the wrong behaviors are reinforced.

Another way of saying it: you get more of what you allow than what you don't. When anything less than radical hospitality takes place, a change of behavior is required that needs to be brought to the attention of those involved *immediately.*

Behaviors to look for to know if there are occurrences of

Radical Hospitality happening in your organization:

- Employees going the extra mile for the customer and each other
- Showing the way rather than pointing the way
- Answering the need rather than merely answering the question
- Considering interruptions as your job rather than as distractions from your job
- Valuing each individual person as worthy of respect, assistance, and care

Businesses that practice radical hospitality with their employees and customers could hang up a sign in their break rooms and on their front doors that states:

We want to know how we can serve you better.

We will listen because your needs are our number one priority.

There is always a seat for you to talk with us.

Radical hospitality also plays an important role in how service employees are supported by management and each other when dealing with abusive customers. There are plenty of stories in the news of employees being verbally abused, threatened, and even physically harmed by out-of-control customers.

I'm personally aware of a situation where an employee was threatened with, "Don't you dare tell me to wear a mask. I'm going to punch that f***ing mask off of your face," and other verbal abuse before the customer finally left the building. The employee was visibly shaken by the interaction and the manager on duty failed to support the employee, telling her to, "Stop acting like a baby...and get back to work."

Not surprisingly, the employee quit on the spot. I've also heard of two other employees from that business that subsequently quit because of how their co-worker was treated.

For radical hospitality to be given to the customer, employees must feel safe and protected in their work. To expect anything else would be foolish.

COVID-19 AND YOUR
FATIGUED CUSTOMER

This is an unprecedented time in the history of business, and the pandemic is likely disrupting your ability to meet your customers' and employees' needs. And as the pandemic lingers, our customers are becoming less patient and willing to comply with mandates including masks and social distancing. And to compound the problem there are copious amounts of misinformation being spread everyday.

Now, perhaps more than ever, your business needs to focus on building customer relationships that will persist beyond the coronavirus. Your approach to customer service and the customer experience must adapt, or your business will face the consequences of not innovating to meet the changing demands.

Your business may be experiencing a shortage of customers - either by government mandate or by fear of the virus. A recent Gallup Poll indicated that 6 in 10 Americans are now "very" (26%) or "somewhat worried" (34%) that they or someone in their family will be exposed to the coronavirus.

What can your business do to strengthen relationships with consumers when social distancing has minimized or eliminated personal interaction?

The article ***Ensure That Your Customer Relationships Outlive the Coronaviru***s (https://hbr.org/2020/04/ensure-that-your-customer-relationships-outlast-coronavirus)s in the Harvard Business Review lists five key strategies to help your business weather the pandemic and preserve the bonds with your customers. My adaptation of the five key strategies are:

Humanize your business

Educate your customers about changes to your business

Assure stability for your employees and customers

Revolutionize your products and services

Think differently to create the future

Let's take a closer look at how you can use each component of the **HEART** strategy in delivering Professional Customer Service:

Humanize your business
Let your customers know that your business understands the dire social circumstances of the pandemic, and that you care more about them than your bottom line during this difficult time.

Empathize with those affected by COVID-19 and spell out the steps your business is taking to help customers, employees, and other stakeholders in this time of uncertainty and unknowns. Your social media sites and customer mailing lists are ideal tools for doing this, as well as your daily interactions with your employees and customers.

Professional customer service means communicating brief, respectful and consistent messages on how your business will help the customer and keep them safe as they do business with you. Think of including phrases like, "Contactless delivery," and, "No customers in the middle seats," and, "Stay safe in your car with our curbside pick-up".

By humanizing your company and showing the customer you care about their wellbeing, you are much more likely to retain their business.

Educate your customers about changes to your business

Keep the customer informed about the changes in your business operation, including new hours, facility closures, staff reductions, customer service availability, ordering options, etc.

You want to be seen as being proactive and motivated by your customers' best interests, not as a business that is a victim of the times or the government mandates.

Also, meet regularly with your employees to craft and create consistent message sharing strategies. Nothing decimates professional customer service more than inconsistent messaging with the employees, which will in turn create inconsistent messaging with your customers. This is a guaranteed way to lose your customers.

By making sure your employees are all on the same page, they will be able to educate your customers and make sure you lead to the same with your customers. That will ultimately lead to less customers - guaranteed.

Assure stability for your customers and employees

Show and tell the customer how your business will continue to provide the products and services they have come to know, expect and love — the defining reasons they patronize your business instead of others.

The pandemic may prevent your business from giving the customers the sense of normalcy that they are desperately craving, but your customer service excellence will show them your business will continue to provide the value that they expect.

For your employees, a similar strategy of communication of the pandemic is that the mindset of "we've always done it that way" is a permanent thing of the past. Businesses will need to focus on helping their employees overcome their fears of potential job loss, less working hours and of safely interacting with the customer.

Honest and forthright communication with your employees will yield similar communication with your customers. If your employees don't have a sense of stability from your business it will be reflected in the experience they offer your customer.

Revolutionize your products and services

This is a time of innovation for your organization! It is simply not good enough to tell your customers that you are open or reopening for business. Get the input of your employees and customers on new products and services that you will offer to meet their needs and solve their problems.

Winston Churchill said, *"Never waste a crisis,"* and that should be your business mantra each and every day that COVID-19 shapes your experiences with your customers and employees. This is an unprecedented time of opportunity. Seize it!

Be the business that injects hope into your customers' heartache, as they see how you are changing and offering ways to make their lives better.

Thinking differently to create the future

It is of the utmost importance to communicate to your employees and customers that your business is making decisions that will shape the future, versus being a victim of the present circumstances. Let's look at two techniques to help you think differently in creating the future of your business.

Assumption Reversal

Assumption Reversal is a powerful technique to help your business overcome the assumptions that are being made about a current situation, project or business model. Too often when we brainstorm, we make assumptions around how something *has* to work or what *has* to be included in it for it to be a success. Those assumptions can often be wrong. Assumption Reversal allows you to take your assumptions and turn them on their head to create something totally new and different. Here's an example of how it works:

Richard James and Maurice James McDonald were the American founders of the first McDonald's restaurant in San Bernardino, California. They were inventors of the "Speedee Service System," now commonly known as "fast food". They used the assumption reversal technique repeatedly in designing their restaurant in 1948. Their goal was to find more efficient ways of serving young working families looking for a cheap meal. Some examples of assumption reversal for their business model included:

- customers arrived by car
- the restaurant design deliberately omitted an interior dining area
- There was no waiting staff; orders were taken in person at the front counter where the food was also delivered
- The brothers designed the kitchen area themselves, integrating their acquired knowledge into an assembly line–style layout that maximized efficiency and output
- The burgers were pre-cooked and kept warm
- There were no plates or silverware given to the customer

All of these attributes for the original McDonald's challenged previously assumed standards in the restaurant industry, and McDonald's restaurants in the 21st century continue to be a leading example of success by the systems put into place for efficiency and interchangeability. By simply following the systems in place, any new hire can build a special-order cheeseburger, make a milkshake or French Fries and serve the customer.

To learn more about the Assumption Reversal technique, invest your time in these resources:

"Assumption Reversal in Pandemic Crisis"
Joker News; posted on YouTube April 14, 2020
https://www.youtube.com/watch?v=sbjmKa6tcMY

"Coronavirus: The Good That Can Come Out of an
Upside-Down World"
Matthew Syed
BBC News; posted March 30, 2020
https://www.bbc.com/news/world-us-canada-
52094332

"Reversing Assumptions Technique"
Michael Michalko, "Think Jar Collective"
https://thinkjarcollective.com/tools/reversing-
assumptions-technique/

Customer Gap Analysis

A customer gap analysis is an analysis that studies the
difference between customer expectations and customer
experiences. With customer service improvement as our
identified area for a gap analysis, we can ask the following
questions:

·   What is the current state of our customer service?

·   What do we want the future state to be?

·   How are we going to close our service gap?

Conducting a gap analysis can help you improve your
customer service efficiency by showing the "gaps" present in
your service model that the pandemic may have exposed or
caused to become more apparent.

Once the analysis is done, you'll be able to focus your
resources, time and energy on those identified areas in order to
improve your service to the customer. Best of all, with the gap

analysis you will be able to implement changes and then use it to measure the successes and failures of those changes.

Tools and information to help you perform a Customer Gap Analysis technique:

Customer Gap Analysis Template
The 5 Gap Model of Service Quality to help you better understand your customers' needs - https://lapaas.com/gap-model-of-service-quality/

MASKS, SOCIAL DISTANCING AND THE OPPORTUNITIES FOR CUSTOMER SERVICE IMPROVEMENT IN A PANDEMIC

As more businesses and government entities are requiring customers to wear masks in their buildings, customer resistance to those mandates and policies continues to rise with sometimes violent conclusions.

Customers in the United States, perhaps more than in any other country, are divided and defiant over wearing a mask and their behaviors are causing businesses and their employees to be faced with difficult decisions. Even worse, some governments are putting the enforcement of their mask mandates on the business owners and management. Truly, a lose-lose situation for everyone involved.

While I could focus on employees being or not being "The Mask Police" in their organizations, instead I will focus on overcoming the challenges of an employee wearing a mask when serving the customer.

First of all, the obvious. Say goodbye to many of the body language cues we normally get from a customers' facial expressions. Those expressions greatly help with reading their feelings and behaviors, and the loss of that nonverbal communication has presented many challenges.
Fortunately, we can still see the customers eyes. A popular saying is "the eyes are the gateway to soul," and they are also a wealth of important information in our customer interactions.

For example, when a customer is squinting, narrowing or widely opening their eyes they are communicating a message to you. To be clear, this is only one piece of information (also known as a tell) and you need to observe other tells from the customer including posture, arm and hand gestures, and torso and leg movements.

The article Understanding Body Language and Facial Expressions https://www.verywellmind.com/understand-body-language-and-facial-expressions-4147228 is a good guide that you can use to sharpen the skill of understanding body language cues.

Another challenge that customer service employees are uncovering is how to effectively communicate with their masks on. As I'm sure you've noticed, we have to speak louder to compensate for the mask and we need to understand that the mask may make it more difficult for us to properly enunciate our words in a way that helps the customer understand us.

Tone of voice also becomes much more critical, and you'll want to remember the little things like slowing down your pace to make sure the customer is understanding you and making sure that you are facing the customer. It can be easy to look down at your computer, a product, or even a piece of paper while you are explaining to them. Become more aware of how you position yourself with the customer.

And just to make the communication dance even more challenging, you will be expected to do all of this while keeping a safe physical distance.

Jamie Matczak, Education Consultant with the Wisconsin Valley Library Service offers excellent advice on customer service when wearing a mask in the YouTube video: *Digital Byte: Communication Tips (While Wearing a Mask)*. https://www.youtube.com/watch?v=B-YLLQ65YYU&t=9s I found the advice given in the video was not only important when serving others while wearing a mask, it was also a great reminder of many of the best practices in customer service.

Social Distancing vs. Physical Distancing

I have been both fascinated and concerned with the phrase *social distancing* - not only for customer service, but for our lives in general. We are social creatures, whether you consider yourself an introvert, extrovert or even an ambivert. I don't believe that we want to be socially distant from others but I do understand the need to be physically distant, and that distinction plays a large role in our ability to communicate.

Professional customer service can fail when we try to be socially distant, especially if we cut off the emotional connection with our customers and colleagues. Losing that connection would be fatal to any business as customers need an emotional connection (kindness, respect, a feeling of being welcomed and valued), especially during these fragile times. For your business to thrive during and after the pandemic, social connection will be critical.

Walt Disney once said *"There are no new ideas"* which is a fascinating quote. How could this incredibly creative and brilliant man who invented and manifested theme parks, animated pictures and so much more claim that even his own ideas were not new?

I think what Walt Disney was saying was that many people may have had the same idea before even if they did not act on it, hence the idea is not new. An example of this would be the patenting of a device we use every day. On March 7th, 1876, Alexander Graham Bell patented his revolutionary new invention - the telephone. Bell and a team of others had worked on this idea while at Boston University beginning in 1873, yet the idea of the telephone was not unique to them. Scientists and engineers in France and Italy had been working on the telephone since the early 1850's.

With regards to social distancing I was not surprised to find that others had similar ideas and concerns to mine about the use of the phrase. Two articles in Psychology Today online specifically highlighted the dangers of socially distancing ourselves from others. Those articles can be found here:

Social vs. Physical Distancing: Why It Matters by Amy Banks - https://www.psychologytoday.com/us/blog/wired-love/202004/social-vs-physical-distancing-why-it-matters

Let's Aim for Physical Rather Than Social Distancing by Kenneth E. Miller Ph.D. - https://www.psychologytoday.com/us/blog/the-refugee-experience/202003/lets-aim-physical-rather-social-distancing

I suggest that now perhaps more than ever in my lifetime that customers need to feel a sense of connection with the people they do business with. And furthermore, the lack of connection many people are feeling is leading to disturbing behaviors from customers that we would not normally see.

The challenge for everyone in customer service management is to clearly communicate the difference between physical and social distancing in the way that business will be done, and to thoroughly explain how everyone in the organization will accomplish that objective. Every business is different, but the customers' needs are the same: connection. An idea to consider is to collaborate with your employees on ways to stay socially connected with the customers and each other despite all the COVID obstacles. This includes employees that are working remotely who may be feeling more isolated than you realize.

The Opportunities for Customer Service Improvements in a Pandemic

"I like to say that crisis creates an opportunity." - Levi Strauss CEO Chip Bergh

In mid-March when the inevitability of COVID became apparent in the United States, my first reaction was to examine and seize the opportunities that would be made available for my online business. I didn't see a lack of need for our training services, I saw an abundance of opportunity.

I also understood that to take advantage of the opportunities of the crisis that my organization would need to make changes in how we operate. This was a somewhat daunting task. We are a small business without the resources of a Levi Strauss, yet I knew that we needed to focus on the things we could control and not worry about what other businesses were doing.

My first step was to reach out to my existing clients and to ask them how we could help them to serve their clients and customers. My next step was to ask them to refer my webinar business to their colleagues.

In a matter of two weeks we were taking on more work from our existing clients and had secured two statewide contracts from new clients. Undoubtedly our reputation of presenting programs that are **P**rofessional, **C**urrent and **I**nteractive (**PCI**) helped us to attract more business, but I knew it was our dedication to radical hospitality that would get us referrals and customer loyalty.

More clients for PCI Webinars meant more customer service interactions each day and we needed to get those interactions right…right away. I spoke with my all remote staff about the need for consistency in the communication of our products and services, and the need of our customers for us to be flexible and adaptable to their needs. Our messaging needed to be consistent and accurate because customer confusion is a service disaster waiting to happen.

More clients also meant that we had to reexamine our systems and processes. We were going to outgrow our current capacity and needed to investigate new technologies to meet the increased demand. These were good problems to have (if there are such things), as it meant that our organization had indeed begun to seize upon the opportunities of the pandemic.

Six months into the pandemic, I am able to share with you three opportunities from personal experience that will help anyone that has the responsibility of serving customers.

Learning - Continuous Improvement

I'm a huge believer in the wisdom contained in the book *The 7 Habits of Highly Effective People* by Dr. Stephen Covey. Habit Number 7 is Sharpen the Saw, which means to improve your skills in some way every day. There are many ways to improve your customer service skills and taking the initiative to learn new techniques, approaches and best practices is something that anyone can do.

Finding the money to access this information is not an obstacle as there are plenty of free learning opportunities online, and of course through your local library. If you don't have a library card or believe that libraries are obsolete, I recommend you think again. In my small library system in Western North Carolina I have access to customer service training through databases including Universal Class and RB Digital. There are opportunities to learn computer skills, classes to improve verbal and written communication skills, time management, learning a different language and many more skills that increase your value as a customer service employee.

As the pandemic continues to spread and businesses are adjusting to an uncertain future, an inevitable truth many people will face is a furlough, reduction in hours or permanent loss of their job.

With all of the unknowns still to come with the pandemic, your best strategy is to become more valuable to your current or future employer. And unlike the daily twists and turns of the pandemic, you are in control of how much time and energy that you want to invest in learning.

This book is filled with links for articles and videos for you to consume to Sharpen Your Saw. You have the opportunity to create your future each and every day.

Increase Your AQ

As businesses continue to explore their options for surviving and hopefully flourishing in the COVID era, they will need their employees to increase their ability to adapt to the changes and uncertainties.

From The Ivey Academy, **Adaptability Quotient (AQ)** is the ability to determine what's relevant, to forget obsolete knowledge, overcome challenges, and adjust to change in real time.

Those with a high AQ demonstrate the following behaviors:

- Open-mindedness. They actively work on managing their unconscious bias to remain open to possibilities
- They actively seek to view situations from the perspectives of others
- They prioritize developing new skills and continually invest in their own learning to better prepare themselves for an uncertain future

Adaptable leaders and employees are better equipped to support their business's needs as they change and grow – and they're in high demand.

https://www.ivey.uwo.ca/academy/blog/2020/02/adaptability-quotient/

What can you do to improve your adaptability to the changing needs of your customers and employer? That should be the question you ask each day before you begin your work.

Here are some suggestions to help you raise your adaptable

quotient:

Lose the "But we've always done it that way!" belief system and behaviors. That mindset not only makes you less than a professional customer service employee, it makes you expendable. And if you are reacting to this by saying "I don't like change", let me say what your employer needs to say: It isn't about you; it's about the customer and the longevity of the business.

Ask for the "why"

Hopefully the days of management telling you, "I told you so, that's why." are coming (or have already come) to an end in your organization. This style of authoritarian management destroys the morale of the employees, which of course is reflected in the experience of the customer. It also scares away the good employees who will find a more collaborative work environment elsewhere.

Anyone that manages or leads others that believes "I told you so" is an acceptable answer to an employee legitimately asking to understand why a decision was made needs to heed these three pieces of advice:

> 1) No one likes to be told what to do (including you, the manager)
>
> 2) You demonstrate a lack of management skills and more importantly, people skills that are critical to team, department and organizational success
>
> 3) Your advancement potential will be limited because your bosses will see the shortcomings of your ability to get the most out of others

As you can see I am very passionate about the importance of "why". Simon Sinek in his popular Ted Talk *How Great Leaders Inspire Action* demonstrates "The Golden Circle", a powerful visual of the differences between the what, how and why in how we communicate with our employees, customers and stakeholders. The powerful phrase *"People don't buy what you do, they buy why you do it"* resonates with me every time I consider a message I want to send to my staff and customers.

Your people connect to you as a leader when they understand the why. Your customers are much more loyal to your business and brand when they connect to your why. *"People don't buy what you do, they buy why you do it."* Write that down on a sticky note and post it somewhere that you will see it each day, and watch as your employees and customers become more invested in your business.

You can view Simon Sinek's Ted Talk here:
https://www.ted.com/talks/simon_sinek_how_great_leaders_i nspire_action

Just as employees deserve the respect of having their "why" questions answered, your customers deserve the same respect too. Professional customer service goes beyond telling the customer the rules or the policy, which normally is not in their favor. To build customer relationships and create more positive customer experiences, we must include the why of a decision and I suggest it be done before the customer asks why.

One of my favorite techniques is the *because* technique. Example: *Unfortunately, we are unable to give you a refund because the product has been damaged.*

Whenever possible, follow up the because with a **suggestion or possible alternatives for the customer.**

Unfortunately, we are unable to give you a refund because the product has been damaged. ***However, you may want to contact the manufacturer directly to discuss your return options. Here is the phone number for their customer support department.***

Make the why your ally in customer situations. You will learn that by explaining the why more effectively, it will reveal hidden opportunities for you to be flexible with the given situation. Your customers won't always agree with the *why* that you give them, but it will be a starting point to exploring other options that may solve the problem at hand and create an even more loyal customer for the business.

Gain Experiences / Share Experiences

I noted earlier in this chapter to need to seize the opportunity to Sharpen the Saw, and while learning is an important first step, applying what you learned is where the true payoff begins.

You are going to be challenged to adapt to new and different customer situations as your organization adjusts to the changing times. It is likely that you are going to need different approaches from what you have used before to be most effective. This is where experience is the most wonderful teacher.

You will try some things with the customer that may not work as well as you would like or possibly something that works too well. If it didn't work the first time, don't give up. Modify your language or your approach. Working with customers is an experiment in building relationships and connections. Learn from your customers' reactions and confidently proceed to your next customer.

Be careful of a technique or approach that seems to work almost every time because it can make you complacent and step out of the moment with your customer. You may also begin to get defensive about your technique when it doesn't work. You might even say to yourself or a coworker that you don't understand why the customer got upset.

I hope that you see that in these situations your focus has shifted from the customer to your technique and somehow the customer relationship has become about you, and not you and the customer.

Please share your experiences with others in your business. Your small customer service victories and near misses will have a greater impact when others learn from them too. Unlike sales, customer service doesn't need to be a competition. As a long-time manager of customer service teams, I can tell you that an employee that collaborates with others is highly regarded as not only a team player, but also as someone an organization will fight to keep when economic times are tough.

Experience is not what happens to you; it's what you do with what happens to you.- Aldous Huxley

CUSTOMER SERVICE CPR

The pandemic has brought many opportunities and challenges to our people working in customer service.

One of the challenges that I feel must be discussed is the pandemics effect on the mental health of our employees. For example, many employees have real fears of contracting the virus by interacting with the each other and their customers. These fears should not be minimized or dismissed. There are many more fears including the loss of their jobs, the closing of the business and a possible loss of hours and wages.

And the challenges I have mentioned do not address the many family-based ones that the employees are facing at home.

The mental health of customer service employees needs our attention. Whether you are a manager, an employee or a customer, I advocate that CPR is greatly needed and welcomed to help people minimize the stressors on their mental health.

CPR = Compassion, Purpose and Resiliency

Compassion

Merriam-Webster defines compassion as a
sympathetic consciousness of others' distress together with a desire to alleviate it.

Customers need more compassion from the people they do business with. Employees need more compassion from the businesses that continue to employ them.

The unknowns and uncertainties of the pandemic have added to the stressors of what for many is already a hectic life where there wasn't enough time in the day to get things done. Routines have been disrupted, habits broken and normalcy...we can't even imagine what that is from day to day.

What we can do to help our customers, our co-workers and businesses to a healthier mental outlook is to be more compassionate. It is to be more sympathetic and as the definition suggests...to have a desire to alleviate other's distress.

It is to care as much or even more about the human side of the business than the rules and policies. It is to use the people skills we have been taught in customer service including listening and understanding with a compassionate perspective. It is about changing our own mental approach to our customers.

For example, instead of saying:

"what's wrong with that person" or;

"I don't understand how someone can say that"

we change our internal dialogue to:

"What happened to that person that caused them to be so upset/angry/distraught right now?"

"I know what they are saying doesn't make sense, how can I best help them right now?"

In reality, it is likely that you will never know what happened to them that caused them to behave the way they are behaving and your best efforts in offering them help may not bring understanding to the situation. But that's okay.

In these situations, the outcome of the conversation or transaction is not what's most important. What is important is that in a difficult moment you chose compassion over judgment. You chose to care instead of walking away or getting frustrated by not understanding.

Look for opportunities to offer more compassion to your customers and coworkers. A kind word or gesture may make a huge difference in their lives.

Purpose

When everything seems to be spinning out of control, there is something powerful about changing your focus to your purpose. Your purpose is your why. Why do you choose to do the work that you do? What motivates you to work in customer service or to manage a customer service team?

When you are most frustrated, most upset or dismayed with your current situation remember that *you are in control of your next thought*. You can choose to continue to feel like things are spinning out of control, or you can choose to change the direction of your thinking. Your purpose can be one of your next thoughts to help you lower your stress, minimize your emotions and to focus on something positive.

Purpose is like a compass to keep you on track when you have lost your sense of balance and direction. It is also one of the most powerful customer service values that we deliver.

Communicating the purpose of our business to our customers is critical. Especially through and after the pandemic we need to communicate why they are important to our business and why our business important to them.

A service or product delivered with purpose builds loyalty and connection with them. As Simon Sinek said in his Ted Talk *How Great Leaders Inspire Action*, *"people don't buy what you do, they buy why you do it."*

Used in the context of the video presentation the word *buy* does not mean purchase, a purchase is an outcome. Buy means connecting with the customer. It means the customer builds a relationship and a trust with your product or service. They grow a fierce loyalty to your business because they relate to and embrace the purpose of your business.

The same is true with employees that buy-in to the purpose of a business. They work harder and are more loyal than someone who finds no purpose in the work they do for a business.

Before your next day of work take time to think about your individual purpose and the purpose of your employer. Does your purpose match theirs? Are you aligned in your belief and in your values with the operations of the business?

Remember to focus on your purpose to help you through the bad days. It helps you to focus on what's important in your life while maneuvering through the ups and downs of the day. And, a few seemingly bad days, or weeks did you ever consider that you may be near a breakthrough of some kind? Consider the quote from the book, *When Things Fall Apart by* Buddhist teacher Pema Chodron:

"When things are shaky and nothing is working, we might realize that we are on the verge of something. We might realize that this is a very vulnerable and tender place, and that tenderness can go either way. We can shut down and feel resentful or we can touch in on that throbbing quality."

Finally, remember to show and tell your customers and coworkers why they are important to you. When you are living on and in your purpose doing the little extra things including kindness and compassion almost become automatic. And those little extra things are noticed and appreciated.

Responsibility

It is easy to blame the pandemic for the chaos many of us are feeling in our lives right now. Yet one of my greatest lessons in life was to stop blaming others for my worries and woes and to take responsibility for my life. I was using blame to be a victim of my circumstances. You may be doing the same thing.

Whatever the circumstances of life you may be experiencing as you read this book, I ask you to look at those circumstances and take responsibility for those that you can. The pandemic is not anyone's fault. How you react to the changes COVID has brought into your life is your responsibility.

Know in your heart that blame is a great deceiver. It deceives us from acknowledging the truth about ourselves and in turn robs us of our potential.

In your customer service work...take responsibility. Take responsibility for your actions and your words. If you make a mistake, own up to it. If you could have done better with a customer, co-worker or in a customer situation acknowledge it.

As a new customer service manager, I took over a team of customer service professionals that had been allowed to blame each other instead of taking responsibility and fixing problems. I immediately took two actions that changed the attitude and expectations of our team work environment.

The first thing I did was to put a banner up in my office and in the break area that read: *This is a blame-free workplace*. I told them in one of our first meetings that the blame-game in our team was over. They were not allowed to blame others to me or any other member of the team. If a team member fell back into the old habit of blame, the team was to redirect the conversation immediately. Venting was fine; blaming was not.

I reinforced this expectation by telling them that actions do have consequences, but most times the consequences would be the secondary conversation. If we had a service failure, we would examine it and determine how we would remedy this and similar future situations. If there were consequences to our actions they would be discussed and fairly implemented.

I also made it clear that one of the quickest ways to gain my respect was to tell me when you made a mistake. Our team motto became: *When you make a mistake, take responsibility for it, learn from it and let it go.*

The second action I took was to tell my team I immediately expected them to stop blaming each other about their workplace problems. Further and when applicable, bring me solutions to the problems that they noticed.

Blaming others is a huge waste of time and energy. I asked them to consider what positive changes we make with that time and energy when it was focused differently.

After a few months of different managerial expectations, the team began to comment on how morale seemed to be better and their work seemed to be less stressful. They also commented that for the first time in years that they felt comfortable talking about problems and solutions with the team instead of being afraid to bring them up.

Take responsibility for your situation. It is one of the most empowering things you will do. Take responsibility to fix a customer service error or situation. To the customer you just might be their hero. To your team and to your manager you may be seen as going above and beyond

To me, you would be someone I am very proud of and that I would respect.

How would taking responsibility change your life? Remember this quote from Nino Quebin *"Your present circumstances don't determine where you can go; they merely determine where you start."*.

And to start you must take responsibility.

FINAL THOUGHTS

Many people that have read earlier drafts of this book have commented that this little book in a bigger context is about changing the culture of an organization. I acknowledge that changing the culture of an organization is an all-hands-on process that can take years to accomplish.

While I would like to believe that professional customer service would indeed become part of your businesses culture, I wrote this book to empower people working in customer service to change themselves, which in turn would have a huge impact on customer relationships and could have an impact on the culture in their organization.

Whether you are in customer service management or supervision, or working on the front lines with the customer, COVID-19 has changed what the customer needs and their expectation of how the service should be delivered.

The pandemic has reminded us of the fragile state of many businesses and the impact of lost revenue on the employment of customer service workers in careers including hospitality, travel and retail.

As I am writing these final thoughts, Disney has furloughed twenty-six thousand employees and the airlines have furloughed sixty thousand more. For those that are in transition or that still have a job, this is your starting point.

Some customer service workers have already begun to re-tool themselves on a new career path. I applaud them for taking the first steps to adapt.

These hard times are a great reminder that some of the most valued skill sets in business are people skills. Upgrading your people and customer service skills may be your biggest advantage in either retaining your current position or in landing your next one.

Now that you have read The Little Book of Professional Customer Service the choice is yours to commit to improve yourself.

The choice to commit to making little improvements in your skills should be seen as a win-win as it will increase your value to the customer, which of course will only make you more valuable to your organization. And there's a personal win for you too as you create more satisfaction in your work.

"Great jobs are made, not found. People often believe they have to make a dramatic change in their work in order to be more fulfilled, whether this means finding a new job or transitioning to a whole new career. In most cases it's important to start by maximizing the contributions you're making within your current work." — Tom Rath, Life's Great Question: Discover How You Contribute To The World

CUSTOMER SERVICE WEBINARS AND WORKSHOPS FROM ANDREW SANDERBECK

https://peopleconnectinstitute.com/customerservice/

Preparing for the Next Wave of Pandemic Fatigued Customers'

The New Basics of Professional Customer Service

De-Escalating Difficult COVID-19 Customer Behaviors

Customer Service on the Telephone and by Email

Managing a Professional Customer Service Team

Professional Internal Customer Service

Raising the Bar! Tools for Continuous Improvement with Your Customer Service Team

The Customer Service Experience

The Quiet Approach for Serving Customers

Successfully Dealing with Harassing Customer Behaviors

No, the Customer Isn't Always Right

Don't Eat the Red Frog

CONTACT ANDREW SANDERBECK

Websites:

www.peopleconnectinstitute.com
www.pciwebinars.com

Email:

andrew@peopleconnectinstitute.com

Phone:

727-409-2239

Linked In

https://www.linkedin.com/in/andrew-sanderbeck-7a11063/

ABOUT THE AUTHOR

Andrew Sanderbeck is a renowned presenter and expert consultant for organizations worldwide. His favorite topics include customer service and retention, creating effective communication habits and management and leadership development. He has presented at national, state and regional conferences, as well as international conferences in the United Arab Emirates and numerous European Countries.

Andrew is the author of two books: The Power of Asking for What You Want and The ABCs of Positive Living, and he has produced more than 50 audio programs including Preparing for the Next Wave of Pandemic Fatigued Customers.

CPSIA information can be obtained
at www.ICGtesting.com
Printed in the USA
LVHW021722230321
682229LV00003B/960